Rock That Body!

How to Gain Total Body Confidence

and

Transform Your Life

The Grieving Heart Series

Aryla Publishing © 2017

www.arylapublishing.com

Visit the site for more information on books by Fiona Welsh *and to be informed of* **free promotions!**

Dedicated to all the body conscious people. We are all different shapes and sizes it's time to love that body!

Please see other books in my series

The Grieving Heart:-

How To Be Strong During A Break Up

How To Deal With Financial Stress

The Great Expectations Of Life

Rock That Body: How To Gain Total Body Confidence

Dealing with Death : Finding Your Way After a Loss

Depression: Dealing With Depression Mental Health Support

Anxiety Dealing With Anxiety & Panic Attacks, Mental Health Support

Business & Home Series:-

How to Make Money Online

Keeping Your Children Safe

Contents

INTRODUCTION   **5**

CHAPTER 1: WHAT IS BODY CONFIDENCE?   **7**

WHY DO WE FEEL BAD ABOUT OUR BODIES?   7

THE DANGERS OF LOW BODY CONFIDENCE   13

CHAPTER 2: THE POSITIVE EFFECTS OF BODY CONFIDENCE, & TACKLING BODY CONFIDENCE ISSUES   **17**

CHANGING YOUR MINDSET   18

CHAPTER 3 – BODY CONFIDENCE TRIGGER TIMES, AND HOW TO DEAL WITH THEM   **21**

IDENTIFYING YOUR TRIGGER   24

CHAPTER 4: HOW TO FEEL GREAT IN YOUR OWN SKIN   **27**

POSITIVE AFFIRMATIONS/MANTRAS   28

DRESS FOR YOUR STRENGTHS   28

DRESS FOR YOU, NOBODY ELSE   28

DISTRACT YOURSELF AND FILL YOUR LIFE WITH FULFILLING ACTIVITIES AND OPPORTUNITIES   29

FOCUS ON HEALTH   30

AVOID COMPARISONS   30

REWARD YOURSELF FOR EVERY POSITIVE CHANGE OR ACCOMPLISHMENT   31

CHAPTER 5 – HEALTH AND WELLBEING   **32**

THE IMPORTANCE OF EXERCISE   35

CHAPTER 6: DIFFERENT BODY SHAPES, AND HOW TO DRESS FOR YOURS   **38**

FEMALE BODY SHAPES   38

MALE BODY SHAPES   40

CONCLUSION   **42**

Introduction

Whether your New Year's resolution has fallen by the wayside, you're busy reading 'beach body' diets, or you're perusing the latest celebrity magazines, you will no doubt come across something that makes you feel a little less than confident in your body.

Male or female, there is more and more pressure piled upon us to look the very best—whether that is thin, curvy, muscly, tanned, toned, or something in-between.

Who decided what 'perfection' was anyway? Is perfection even real? Why is being overweight considered less desirable than being skinny? Who told us that you must be waxed and preened within an inch of your life, or otherwise you're not looking after yourself?

Life is difficult enough already, we don't need these added pressures coming into play.

If you've ever looked in the mirror and felt under pressure to look a certain way, or you've felt upset about your weight, hair, skin or some other part of your body, then this book is for you.

I say that life is far too short to feel lacking in the appearance department, and whilst you might be rolling your eyes and thinking, *here we go again, it's what's on the inside that counts*. Let me tell you one thing—I have lived this body confidence nightmare, and though nobody ever comes out of it 100% super-confident, or never having an off day, there are many ways you can learn to love what you have, feel confident, and radiate it all on the outside.

Yes, seriously.

If you're from the UK, you will know who Gok Wan is. If you're not from the UK, Mr Wan is a TV personality who took everyday women—perhaps overweight or underweight, or somewhere in between—basically those who had lost all confidence in their appearance and needed a helping hand. Like a fairy godmother sent from Cinderella, Gok Wan took them on a journey of self-discovery. By the end of it, said women were looking and feeling like a million dollars, without the need for cosmetic surgery or drastic diets.

Consider this book your personal Gok Wan for the current day.

You can read the news and tell yourself that 'life is too short', and really it is, but unless you can change your mindset and begin to feel confident on the inside, you're not going to put that idea into practice in a very effective way. You need to change what you think, shut out the anxieties and doubting voices in your head, and stick it to the haters.

I've done it, and believe me, if I can do it, anyone can.

So, if you're reading this introduction and wondering what I've got up my sleeve, then read on, you might be very surprised indeed. If you're not too sure, read on anyway; by the end of this book, my goal is that you'll have a totally new outlook on body confidence, and you'll be well on your way to forging your own breakthrough, one which will leave you radiating health, wellness, and happiness from the inside out.

Shall we begin?

Chapter 1: What is Body Confidence?

We hear the term 'body confidence' so often these days, but how many of you really know what it is?

Confidence is something we exude, something we feel, not something we can see. When we feel confident we are ready to take on the world, but confidence comes in many different levels. You can be mildly confident, or you can be over-confident; over-confidence is basically arrogance, and that is not something you need in your life! With that in mind, the key is to find the perfect spot in between that provides a level of confidence that allows you to feel comfortable in your own skin, and helps you take on new opportunities and challenges as they arise in life.

When it comes to our bodies however, most of us suffer from negative thoughts and demons as far as our appearance is concerned. Body confidence is about not being overly bothered about the 'norm', or what is 'supposed to be', and instead, simply being with what you've got. This is not to say that you won't ever have those days where you feel a bit fat, or are focused on a part of your body that you perceive to be flawed, but these days don't last, they simply pass by as part of a natural flow of life.

When you are body confident, you are happier, it really is that simple.

Why do we Feel Bad About Our Bodies?

We should mention at this point that many people associate body confidence issues with females only, but that is really not the case; men find it just as hard to love their bodies as women do, it's just that the women's issues tend to be emphasized more in the media.

So, why is it that most of us have a body confidence issue of some kind?

There are many reasons for this, we'll start with this. How many times have you picked up a celebrity gossip magazine and gone straight to the 'what were they thinking' page, or something similarly titled, showing pictures of celebs on the beach or at a gathering. The focal point of the page is a big red circle drawn around a certain part of their body that the magazine has decided is less than desirable.

It could be a patch of cellulite, it could be a waxing gone wrong, a bad hair day, or that the magazine deems them to be too skinny, it could be absolutely anything. The magazine has determined there is something fundamentally wrong with that particular celebrity's body and has decided to tell the world.

Now, you pick up that magazine and read it yourself, and immediately start to feel bad about the fact that you have cellulite for example, too. Then what? You start to think that having cellulite is abnormal! The reality is that you will struggle to find one woman on the planet who doesn't have a certain amount of cellulite on some part of their body since it is as normal as breathing, it's just that some know how to hide it!

Guys are also bombarded with pictures of bulging biceps and other so-called desirable muscle groups, but what if that particular guy reading the magazine just doesn't have the body frame to take those muscles? They're left feeling inept, unmanly and bad about their appearance, simply because a magazine has decided that unless you have muscles, your body isn't good enough.

Who decided these things?

I say stop it!

Society has given us a set of appearance rules that we have to abide by, otherwise we class ourselves as ugly, fat, thin, hairy, lanky, and the list goes on. Who says that being curvy isn't beautiful? Of course it's beautiful! Look at Marilyn Monroe! She was one of the most desirable women on the planet in her day, and she has curves to die for!

Who says you *have* to have bulging biceps and pecs that dance? They might work for Arnie, but does every single person on the planet find Arnie good looking? Probably not! Everyone is different, and we should celebrate our differences, rather than compare ourselves to others.

The main reasons that we have developed body confidence issues are:

Social Media

I am quite renowned amongst my friends for having a downer attitude about social media. That's not to say that I don't find Facebook extremely entertaining most of the time, and for work and keeping in touch with family and friends, it's great. However, it's used for the wrong reasons far too much for my liking, and as far as comparisons are concerned, this is the main one.

Think about it—you sit there idly of an evening, wasting half an hour before bed checking your Facebook timeline or your Instagram. You see a picture of your friend on the beach, looking fantastic. You automatically start to compare your belly to hers, and you feel fat. If you're a guy, you start to check your friend's impressive six pack, and you lament the fact that you don't have one.

Now, one thing you need to remember is this—Instagram allows us to airbrush our appearance until we look like Beyonce on her best day, or Brad Pitt at his gorgeous peak. There are apps you can download to slim your face, contour your make up, slim down your legs, and perk up your boobs—all without having to leave your sofa. How do you know that your friend hasn't done exactly that on the posted the photo which is currently making you feel sub-standard?

I know this happens because I've done it! I've taken a selfie and I've Instagrammed the life out of it, until I look like I've had a makeover with the Kardashian's best beauty crew. I gathered comments telling me I looked amazing, but they didn't really hit home because I knew that face wasn't really mine anymore. Did that photos make my friends feel jealous for a second? I'm not bigging myself up here but it probably did, because we all compare ourselves to others, whether we realise we're doing it or not.

Social media has made it far too easy to airbrush not just our faces, but our lives, in order to make them look perfect, when the truth is that nothing is perfect. Then we feel bad about ourselves because we think that we're lacking something, but the truth is that we're all on an even footing, whether we realise it or not.

Social media rant over.

The Press & Magazines

We touched upon this issue earlier, the pictures you see of celebs having their faults pointed out for everyone to see.

Whether you think they deserve it or not (they don't, incidentally), these celebs are still human and they have faults just like everyone else. The only difference is that these people have a team of beauticians and stylists at their disposal, and that is why they look other-worldly most of the time. It's downright impossible to expect to look as sleek and glossy in the real world, not unless you wake up at the crack of dawn for your morning makeover routine—ain't nobody got time for that!

You don't often realise this point when you're having a bad body day, because you will be off again comparing yourselves to these unrealistic ideals—and you will always come out on the negative side as a result.

I remember watching a film a few months ago, I can't remember which it was. There was a scene where a girl had just woken up in the morning. I can remember looking at her and thinking *why does she look like that when she wakes up, I look like a gargoyle with panda eyes and gravity-defying hair.* I asked my friends and they basically told me they looked the same as me; I felt reassured, that's for sure.

We are comparing ourselves to a picture we are force-fed to believe is real by the media, but the truth is that this is nothing but fantasy, provided by an entity trying to sell magazine. If you can remember that fact, you're made for life.

Comparisons

We have talked about comparisons but this is so important that it deserves a section of its own. We don't all have the same body type, we have our own genetics to deal with. That means that if your friend has bulging muscles and a six pack, they were either genetically blessed, or they spend an awful lot of their time at the gym. Similarly, the friend who can eat whatever she likes and never puts on weight (yet probably still complains she's fat) is just blessed with a metabolism which grants her this favour in life. The rest of us only need to gaze at a slice of cake in order to feel it bulging on our thighs.

This is a trade off in life, and whilst it's still a mystery to me, I've learnt that there is no point in getting down about the fact that you can't burn off your food as quickly as your friend.

General Negativity

Unless you are a super-confident person with a hugely positive attitude, it's likely that you feel negative a lot of the time. This is something you can work on, and we're going to cover this issue a lot more in a future chapter, because it's so key to being body confident.

When someone gives you a compliment related to your body, such as you look great, or look like you lost weight, do you take it and say 'thank you', or do you say 'oh no, I feel so fat lately'. It's likely that you utter the latter, because for some very odd reason, we're hard-wired to deflect compliments, almost as though we feel they will burn us. This is wrong! We should be accepting these kind words and not silently wondering if they're making fun of us, or if they really mean them.

The Dangers of Low Body Confidence

This book isn't purely to help you feel more confident and joyous when you bust out the swim-shorts or bikini on the beach this summer, it's about helping you to feel great in your own skin, whether you're wearing your pyjamas or you're suited and booted for a big event. This book is also designed to keep you from falling into the pitfalls of low body confidence, because it's a dark and murky road to embark on.

The dangers of having poor body confidence range from simply feeling terrible about the way you look, making you not want to go out and enjoy yourself, missing opportunities and not taking well-meaning compliments, to even more severe effects, such as anxiety, depression, body dysmorphia, and eating disorders.

We're going to talk about these negative effects because it's important to understand the depth and severity of what having poor body confidence and can do to a person. From there you can be forewarned, and embark on the journey towards feeling comfortable in the body you were born with.

Let's check out these negative effects of poor body confidence in more detail.

Depression
We hear so much about depression in the news, but the bottom line is that it is often caused by poor confidence overall, including body confidence. Depression can range from feeling low for no reason whatsoever, to prolonged feelings of more severe upset. Depression is not something to joke about, and it isn't something to take lightly. Once you begin on this road, it can be very hard to get off it.

Anxiety
Anxiety is often linked with depression, but it can very easily stem from having low self-esteem. Anxiety is a feeling of constant worry and thinking of the worst case scenario; anxiety sufferers are experts at taking a mole-hill and turning it into a mountain, but these thoughts are

seemingly uncontrollable to the sufferer. Anxiety is a very scary and upsetting condition, and suffering from depression is often a pre-curser to developing anxiety also.

Body Dysmorphia

Most people who have very low body confidence have a degree of body dysmorphia. This is when they look in the mirror and see something different to what everyone else sees. For example, they might be a totally healthy weight and look great to everyone else, but when that person looks in the mirror they see someone overweight, someone who needs to lose excess pounds, for example. It doesn't have to be about weight, it can be about any part of the body, but the bottom line is that they see something which isn't real.

Eating Disorders

This is a very well documented area, something which has been in the news for years, and we're talking about conditions such as anorexia, bulimia, and having general issues with food overall. These disorders can range from mild, e.g. a problem with eating certain foods, to something extremely serious and life-threatening, in the case of anorexia and bulimia.

Anorexia is when a person basically starves themselves and they often have a large degree of body dysmorphia to go alongside it, which fuels the obsession with getting thinner and thinner. Bulimia is when a person binge eats, then doesn't eat at all, and then binges again, before making themselves sick to avoid digesting the calories. Both are extremely serious.

Obsessions With Plastic Surgery

Again, if someone develops an obsession with going under the surgeon's knife to achieve perfection, it's often the case that they are suffering from body dysmorphia. When one thing is 'fixed', they will be content for a short time, before fixating on another area of the body that they think isn't perfect and needs another procedure. This is a never-ending circle which costs an extreme amount of money and can be dangerous for the body and mind overall.

These conditions and problems are all basically down to not feeling comfortable, content, and happy with your own body. It's very easy to say 'just be happy with what you've got', because we mentioned earlier in this chapter, we are bombarded with images of what we are 'supposed to be', without having the stand-point of being individual and beautiful regardless. If we were all the same, life would be very boring indeed.

These social pressures are damaging to everyone, but particularly to young boys and girls. The teenage years are so impressionable that they are dangerous times for these body confidence issues to arise. It is our responsibility to help promote the importance of body confidence, so that future generations don't have to suffer from the same past as many of us have had.

From a personal point of view, I have watched my young niece struggle with her weight and appearance, to the point where I now feel she is too thin. When asked about why she feels she is fat (she certainly isn't), she always compares herself to others. The bottom line is that my niece comes from a long line of curvy women, me included, and fighting against your genetics and nature really isn't a fun game to play—it's a losing game in many ways.

This chapter is designed to help you realise that the problem of low body confidence is a serious one, and something which needs to be tackled. If you are nodding your head and recognising your own situation in this chapter, then you are certainly encouraged to read on and figure out your own body confidence demons. We all feel less than our best some days, but if that feeling goes on and applies to most days, then it's really time to hit those confidence issues on the head.

Chapter 2: The Positive Effects of Body Confidence, & Tackling Body Confidence Issues

Well, sure enough, the last chapter was rather negative, explaining all about problems associated with poor body confidence, but this chapter has a much lighter tone. It's important to balance up the lows with the highs, so let's check out why a higher level of body confidence is a great thing, and why we should celebrate our bodies.

If you've ever seen the movie Bridget Jones's Diary, you will definitely know the scene where Bridget hears those words that every woman waits for— "... just the way you are". This is basically an acceptance of Bridget's womanly curves, her ditzy nature, and is an indication that she doesn't need to change... because she is perfect as she is.

How many times have you wanted to hear that said to you? Man or woman, this is something that everyone wishes for, because why should you change? You're unique, there is no-one like you, and nobody has the same body as you.

You'll probably also have heard that 'the body is a temple', and yes it is. Your body is capable of such wonderful things; women bring life into the world, men give life, why are we putting ourselves down? We're amazing creatures, whether we're skinny, curvy, overweight, average, or anything else.

Body confidence has the following majorly positive effects:

- We feel more content and happier overall.
- We try new fashions with an open mind, which may suit us wonderfully well.
- Body confidence increases overall confidence.
- We are more likely to take opportunities, otherwise avoided.

- We are likely to be much healthier as a result.
- There is a lower chance of depression and anxiety

The bottom line is that if we are happy with the way we look, without constantly striving for an idea of perfection that doesn't even exist, we are likely to feel more confident in ourselves overall. This means we are more likely to strive to reach for our dreams, and take opportunities as they come up in our lives.

If you avoided a swimming costume, bikini, or swim-shorts in the past, this might mean you also steered clear of the beach or pool as well. This means you've missed out on something amazing, and that is no way to live your life.

Body confidence is a wide-reaching subject, and one which can have major advantages.

Changing Your Mindset

In order to breed confidence, you need to assess the situation, accept it, and see it from a different perspective. Body confidence isn't about going on a crash diet, it's not about reaching a certain weight, and it's not about Botox and all that jazz, it's about self-acceptance, and that really only comes from within.

First things first, what is it about yourself that you don't like? Is it your weight? Is it your hair? Is it your nose? Is it your legs? What exactly is it that you can really pinpoint as the cause of your body confidence issues? You might struggle to answer this question at first, because you might come up with a few reasons, but it's important to really pinpoint the most obvious and important ones first.

Once you have that answer, look at this rationally. Do you really need to change anything, or is it just what you perceive to be a fault? Ask someone you trust, someone you know is going to tell you the truth and not mess you around—ask them what they think your best features are and what they think are your worst. Does their answer measure up with yours?

Of course, if the issues involves needing to do something for your general health, then go for it; e.g. if you need to lose weight then do it, but do it in a healthy and effective way—crash diets do nothing good, and a lot of bad. If you can't change the issue that is causing you the headache, then it really comes down to acceptance.

Changing your mindset is the key.

Try this exercise.

- Look in the mirror and assess your appearance.
- Start at the top of your head and work down slowly.
- Note the things you like about yourself.
- Note the things you don't like about yourself, and make sure that you come up with an even number for both.
- Now, the things you like about yourself, really focus on them—can you dress yourself in a different way, to flaunt or otherwise emphasize those positive assets about yourself?
- The things you don't like about yourself, can you change them? Can you hide them?
- From the things you like about yourself, create a mantra, e.g. I have beautiful eyes, and repeat this to yourself over and over. Write this mantra down and stick it to your fridge or your bathroom mirror
- Every time you feel yourself slipping into negativity in terms of thinking and focusing on the things you don't like about yourself, repeat the mantra several times. The idea is to refocus your brain, until the positive becomes the first thing you think of, not the negative.

Focusing on positives, rather than negatives, takes time and it takes practice, but it is something that can change your life in so many ways. For instance, if you have always been a glass half empty, rather than half full, type of person, you could use this exercise to bring more positivity into all aspects of your life. This will bring you more happiness and open doors for you, because your positive outlook will force you to try new things. It's not just about your body!

Chapter 3 – Body Confidence Trigger Times, and How to Deal With Them

There are certain times throughout the year, and in our lives overall, where we will find it harder to be body confident than at other times. This is totally normal, but it is how you deal with these times that determines which will help you come out the other side, without feeling substandard or upset.

These times are personal, but they could include such times as:

- Beach holidays
- Weddings
- Special occasions, such as nights out, engagements, family gatherings
- After the birth of a child
- Christmas and other seasonal times when people come together and food is central to the celebrations
- New Year
- Certain birthday milestones in life

There are probably other trigger times in your life that you can pinpoint, because this is totally personal. For me it was when my best friend got married and I was a bridesmaid. I was assigned a beautiful red dress to wear, but I just felt huge, in fact I felt massive. Of course, I wasn't that massive, though I did need to lose weight (and went on to do so), but I certainly didn't look half as big as I thought I did. I realise this now, but at the time I thought there was something hideously wrong with the way I looked, and it put a downer on the whole event for me.

The plus point is that I used the way I felt that day to push me to lose the weight I needed to lose, and gain the body confidence that I have now. I'm not going to lie, I don't look in the mirror every single day and think 'wow, check out that body', because I still have flaws, everyone does, but I have learnt to accept my body for the wonderful miracle that it is, and I do my very best to avoid comparing myself to others. I learnt how to dress for my body shape, something we will go on to talk about in more detail shortly, and I used that trigger time to push me towards a more positive place.

This is what you need to do.

You'll know when you're experiencing a trigger, because your feelings will change. For instance, you may become nervous or start dreading that beach holiday coming up, rather than looking forward to it with the joy that you had when you first booked it. You start to forget all the fun things you're going to do, and that wonderfully warm sunshine beating down on you, and instead, all you can focus on is the fact that you have to bare more skin than you normally would, and you have to wear considerably less clothing on the beach.

This is totally normal; for the first few days of a beach holiday, most people start to dread the initial 'strip down', but usually once that is over, you forget it all and start to enjoy the sunshine and holiday fun. What you need to avoid is letting that feeling extend to the point where you don't enjoy your holiday at all. What was the point in going if you're going to feel that way?

A good solution to the beach issue is to purchase a swimsuit/bikini/pair of swim-shorts that flatter your body and make you feel good, rather than just going for the latest trends. This will give you confidence and you won't have the same severe trigger effects that you would have otherwise experience. For instance, if you really don't like your stomach (the most pinpointed part of the body that causes upset), then you don't have to show it. Just because Cosmopolitan magazine says that spotty bikinis are bang on trend, it doesn't mean you have to wear one! You could go for a tankini, which covers the areas you're not happy with, or you could go for a plunging swimsuit instead, and turn the attention to that fantastic cleavage instead.

This works for the guys also—you don't have to wear Speedos (God forbid!), you can go for baggy basketball-type swim-shorts, and if you don't want to take your shirt off, well, you don't have to. There are no rules, it's about being comfortable and happy in the situation, no matter what anyone else thinks.

Another trigger point for me has always been the New Year celebrations. I think it's because we all put so much emphasis on trying to be a 'new me' for January, and that usually includes transforming body shapes and losing weight. It's not realistic to suddenly change everything about your life when the clock strikes 12 on a fresh year, and it took a lot of mindset changing for me to realise this. Instead of vowing to transform myself into a look akin to Cindy Crawford on a particularly amazing day, I changed the resolutions I made into something more easily achievable, e.g. I vowed to save a little of my wages every month and go on holiday somewhere amazing at the end of the year. Swapping my body-focused resolutions into something much more enjoyable and achievable took the pressure off, and I didn't experience that sinking feeling as January progressed and my waistline didn't get any smaller.

In our next chapter we're going to talk about how to feel good in your own skin, and again, much of that is about mindset training. You have to learn to think differently.

I think a lot of this comes with age in many ways, because I was much more body focused in my 20s, and much less so now that I am in my 30s. Of course, I still want to look nice, and I try my best, but you know what? I have learnt that life is too short to focus on the fact that I cannot rock a mini skirt because of my cellulite, and instead, I have learnt that skinny jeans are a wonderful invention! I have decided to focus my time and attention on things that make me happy and result in a smile, instead of trying to look nice for others or achieve some tabloid standard. I don't need it. They don't do it for me, why should I do it for them?

Identifying Your Trigger

What is it that makes you feel lacking in body confidence? Is it an everyday kind of deal, or is it something that happens at certain times, on certain occasions? Think about this carefully and identify your trigger. Sometimes it can be that you feel increased body angst when you are around a certain person.

This happened to me and I found it rather distressing. I have a friend who has what I always perceived to be the perfect body. She was curvy yet slim, she had long, glossy brunette hair which never seemed to look greasy, even if she didn't wash it for two days, and she had bright blue eyes that didn't need mascara to give them definition. I hated her in some ways, but most of the time I loved her, because she was such a great person.

Not fair, right?

What I didn't realise at the start was that she had undergone a lot of body confidence issues in her past, because she had always been underweight, and as such she had been flat chested. This caused her issues and made her unhappy so she embarked on a nutrition programme to help her gain weight, and she actually had a subtle breast enlargement, to help with her confidence.

She looks amazing, I admit this freely, but the thing is, she still doesn't believe it. She thinks she is too short now, and there's nothing you can do about that!

This taught me that even those you think are 'perfect' have issues of their own.

The problem occurred when I didn't know about any of this, and was still getting to know her as a person. She was what I thought to be perfect in appearance, and she received a lot of admiring glances from the opposite sex. Whenever we went out, or whenever we went to the beach, I compared myself to her and felt completely and utterly lacking. It got to the point where I didn't want to go with her anymore, because it made me feel so bad.

What type of friend was I?

When we actually sat together and she talked about her life, the realization that body issues are universal dawned on me. This is when I started to realise that I needed to change the way I looked at her and how I felt when I was around her. The problem was me, not her.

It might be that you have someone in your life who makes you feel this way too. I would advise you to do some mindset changes, instead of avoiding spending time with them. You never know what kinds of battles people are fighting on the inside, and this is a lesson that is worthwhile learning overall, not just in your efforts to kick-start your body confidence levels.

Once you know your triggers, you can work towards minimising the effects and putting into place a change of mindset, or a few routine tools, to stop it becoming such an issue. Where body confidence is concerned, it's mostly about appearance, but it's also about what you perceive inside. If you feel good on the inside, it shows on the outside, and vice versa.

Now you know what causes your issues to peak, let's talk about how you can learn to feel great in your own skin.

Chapter 4: How to Feel Great in Your Own Skin

Throughout this book so far we have talked about the types of situations which can make you feel lacking in body confidence, we've covered what body confidence is, and why it is important, as well as the negative effects that an issue with body confidence can bring. Now it's time to get practical.

This chapter will discuss how to feel good in the skin that you have. Now, if you need to make changes for your general health, like you need to gain because you're underweight, or lose weight because you're overweight to the point of it impacting your health or wellbeing, then this is something you can work towards on a practical level; our next chapter covers that in more detail. The key here however is that any changes you make in this regard, should be because YOU want to make them, for YOUR personal reasons, nobody else's.

It's also important to realise that you are unique, there is no-one else out there like you, and there shouldn't be either! Do you want to be a carbon copy of someone else? No! You are a wonderful human being on the inside and the outside, and it's about time you realised this fact! Once you come to terms with the realisation that you are an individual, and that you don't have to be like someone else, then you will find this whole journey so much easier.

I always used to compare myself to other people, to the point where I used to model myself on them. It wasn't until I was in my mid-20s that I really realised this was pointless. Learning to love yourself and the person you are on the inside is the biggest key to feeling confident in life no matter what, whether that's about your ability to do your job, to conduct healthy relationships, or regarding your body and image.

So, let's check out a few body confidence boosting tips to try.

Positive affirmations/mantras

We mentioned this earlier in the book, but it's certainly worth mentioning again, such is its power. For this, you need to identify your strengths, e.g. you have a nice cleavage, you have impressive abs, you have nice eyes, your hair is shiny, people always compliment you on your legs. From there, you need to also pick as many strengths that are personality-focused, to avoid becoming too attached to the way you look, so you could think about your sense of humour, your drive, your ability to do your job well, the fact that you are kind, or generous. Turn these strengths into a mantra that you can repeat to yourself over and over whenever a negative thought starts to sneak its way into your mind. This is going to take time, but banishing negativity is the key to confidence overall.

Dress for your strengths

If you don't like your legs, you're never going to feel great showing them off, so instead of doing that, show off a part of your body that you do like. If you don't like your upper arms, wear short sleeves and instead wear a skirt or shorts, if you hate your feet, don't wear sandals! It's not particularly difficult to understand, if you don't like something you can simply distract attention from that area and turn it to a part that you love to show off.

Dress for you, nobody else

Find out what suits you and what you like, and then dress yourself according to that. You don't have to dress for anyone else, especially if it makes you feel uncomfortable.

Feeling happy in your own skin is only going to be achieved by liking what you are wearing, instead of forcing your body into a fashion that suits someone else, but isn't tailored for you. There is no fashion on this planet that suits every single person; for instance, body con dresses were not made for me, and whilst I sometimes wish they were, I just don't even bother looking at them anymore, and instead dress myself in pretty skater dresses, which suit me so much better.

On the flip side, my sister is not someone who can get away with skinny jeans, she knows it, I know it, so she doesn't even bother; instead, she looks downright fantastic in bootcut jeans and she rocks them perfectly! I look ridiculous in boot cut jeans—this is a prime example of how we are all different, but that doesn't make anyone's appearance any better than yours.

Distract yourself and fill your life with fulfilling activities and opportunities

What would you rather have—a life that makes you smile, laugh, and is full of opportunities that bring you happiness, or would you rather just look great? Being skinny does not bring happiness, having a fulfilling life does. Being ripped with muscles does not bring success, working hard does. There are many drop-dead gorgeous models out there who are so beautifully blinding to look at, but on the inside, well, there's not a lot going on. That's not to say all of them of course, there are also many models who are beautiful, smart and have great personalities too, but not all of them. This is proof that it's what inside that counts more than anything else at all.

Instead of focusing on getting skinnier, curvier, or more muscled, you need to focus on filling your life with happy activities, and trying to better yourself in terms of work, family, relationships, etc. Unless you want to spend your days in front of the mirror admiring the fact you managed to get the perfect body, without actually doing anything else with your life, the way forward is to fill your days with fun and fulfilment.

Focus on health

The single most important thing about your body is that it is healthy, not what it looks like. The ironic thing is that when you start to focus mostly on how healthy you are, and keeping yourself in that state, your appearance will glow and sparkle without even trying!

How you are on the inside, shows on the outside, so this means drinking plenty of water, not smoking, avoiding excessive alcohol, eating a healthy and balanced diet, maintaining the best weight for your particular body type, exercising regularly, etc. If you're not sure what weight you should be, it's time to find out your BMI. BMI means Body Mass Index, and this basically tells you the weight range you should be in for your height. Maintaining this means you are much more likely to be healthy, and therefore avoid potential health problems in the future, such as heart problems, diabetes, stroke, cholesterol issues, obesity, etc.

Avoid comparisons

How many times are we going to mention this? Plenty more! This is because avoiding comparisons is such a vitally important part of grabbing body confidence in your life. You can't be like someone else, because you're not them, and they're not you. If you try and emulate someone else, you're just a carbon copy, a fake. Besides, how do you know someone else isn't admiring and trying to be like you? Focus on being the best you can be, with the tools and features that you have. I guarantee you this is the ideal way to feel much more confident in your body and in yourself in general.

I used to compare myself to so many people, but I've now come to realise that I am talented, kind, generous, and selfless, which is so much more important than being able to rock a body con dress without a few bulges here and there. I've even come to realise that my bulges are quite cute in some lights, provided I wear a pair of Spanx! See, I can even laugh at it!

If you're finding avoiding comparisons hard, try having a break from social media for a few weeks—this is the number one reason we compare ourselves to others. Cut out Facebook, Twitter, Snapchat, and Instagram in particular, and instead work on yourself, and only you. See how you feel at the end of it, and if you want to, you can slowly reintroduce social media into your life again, but probably limit it a little, for your own confidence and sanity.

Reward yourself for every positive change or accomplishment

Whenever you have a breakthrough, reward yourself. This could be a night out with friends, it could be a chocolate bar, or it could be something big, like booking a holiday. Whatever it is, make sure that it makes you smile, and that it is something you can look at and enjoy, reminding you of why you literally rock.

Remember my example of saving up cash every month and booking a holiday, rather than deciding to go on a weight loss journey as a New Year's resolution? The ironic thing is that the motivation to go on this beach holiday pushed me towards a healthy lifestyle, and the reward at the end of it was that fantastic holiday in Thailand. It's something I enjoyed massively, and will always remember. Of course, your reward doesn't have to be something so huge, it can be buying yourself a new pair of shoes, or a pair of tickets for your team's latest match.

Every time you achieve something, be it something at work, managing to speak to that guy or girl you've been lusting over for weeks, or something like stopping smoking for two weeks, reward yourself and make yourself feel even more great. Every small thing requires celebration.

Another way to push your body confidence higher is by dressing for your particular body shape, but we are going to cover that in detail in a later chapter. For now, simply know that we are all born with different pre-defined body shapes, and whilst it's possible to change them with exercise and diet, going totally against nature is a job which is high maintenance at the very least. In order to really look your best, you have to identify the shape you are, embrace it, and dress it in the best way possible. I have an hourglass shape, and believe me, it's caused me a headache on more than one occasion, but I now know how to dress my curvy shape and look great, rather than trying to pour my curves into something that is made for a more athletic body shape.

Try these methods to feel great in your own skin just for a short while and see if you notice the difference. Not all of these ideas will work for you, because everyone is different, and different things work for different people, but from there you will be able to identify what really does do wonders for your body confidence, and you can use that method to further push yourself towards contentment.

Chapter 5 – Health and wellbeing

One thing which is tied so intrinsically with body confidence, is health and wellbeing. If you're not healthy, you will find it impossible to be body confident, because your body is going to rebel!

It's vital to be healthy, for obvious reasons, but on the journey towards body confidence it's so easy to be side-tracked. For instance, crash dieting is a very dangerous road to go down, and can lead to terrible health problems. Remember we talked about eating disorders in an earlier chapter? Having issues with food is not a healthy thing, and it will not only play havoc on your body, but it will also tricks on your mind and your perception of how you look— basically, there is no happiness to be found down that road.

So, how can we reach and maintain optimum health and wellbeing?

Okay, first things first, do you need to lose weight? Do you need to gain weight?

This is an issue we will cover first, and we will do so together.

If you need to lose weight or gain weight, it's always a good idea to seek nutritional advice from a trusted healthcare professional. There are so many fad diets out there that it's impossible to know which one is best for you—if you speak to someone who knows what they are talking about, they will give you advice on the vitamins and minerals you need in your diet on a daily basis.

- Eat a variety of fruits and vegetables every day
- Drink plenty of water

- Never skip meals
- Make sure you eat breakfast
- Cut out smoking
- Cut out drinking to excess
- Avoid sugary, processed foods and drinks. Yes, that means diet drinks too, because they are *really* not good for you. I used to drink a lot of Diet Coke, and I thought I was doing myself a good thing here, because I wasn't drinking the full calorie version. Imagine how surprised I was when the moment I stopped drinking it, I actually lost several pounds from that change alone! Water and sugar-free juice is always the best way to go.
- Exercise regularly—This doesn't have to be a huge gym session, it can be something as simple as going for an evening walk with a friend a couple of times a week, walking to work instead of driving, taking the stairs instead of the lift, joining an exercise class once a week, etc.
- Make sure you get your daily quota of protein in your diet, as this is vital to the smooth functioning of your body, and avoid saturated fats, which clog up your arteries and cause major health problems.
- Don't scrimp on sleep, this is a necessity, not a luxury!

As you can see, there is nothing particularly difficult to understand here, and there is no need to embark on a complicated diet of red days, green days, counted calories, weighed amounts of food, and everything else which boggles your mind. Eating isn't a complicated matter, exercise doesn't need to be measured to extremes—simply live your life in a healthy and balanced way, and your overall wellbeing will thank you for it.

If you need to change your weight, either up or down, make sure you do this in a healthy way, rather than in an extreme way. One thing I would certainly advise against is weighing yourself too often.

When I was on my weight loss journey I became a little too obsessed with the scales; I used to weigh myself every single morning, without fail. If I didn't do this, I felt out of control. If I had put on even one pound, I was not happy for the rest of the day; obviously, if I'd lost one pound, I was ecstatic! What I didn't realise was that it was entirely normal for my body to fluctuate up and down by a few pounds throughout the week, and it didn't mean that my diet wasn't working! Weighing daily actually ruined my life in a lot of ways, because I simply wasn't happy for most of the time; I even took my scales with me on a weekend caravan holiday!

For that reason, I would advise you to stick to weighing yourself only once a week, giving yourself a set day, and avoiding doing it at any other time. This is the only way to give yourself an accurate assessment of your gains or losses.

The Importance of Exercise

Exercise is a vital part of keeping us healthy and mobile for as long as possible, but it's important to try and slip this into your life in a way that makes it enjoyable. If you've joined a gym in the past, signed up with the best of intentions, and then found that you just slowly stop going as often, before not going at all (even though you end up paying the subscription every month when you're not even using it), then you probably don't enjoy that type of exercise. Does that mean you don't enjoy any exercise?

No!

I did the exact same thing with the gym, I just didn't the program or the atmosphere. I tried another gym and I felt the same. Whilst I was stuck with a rather annoying year-long subscription, I learnt my lesson, and instead I decided to start a Zumba class with a friend.

I loved it!

I can now shake my rather sizeable booty in the way that it was intended to be shook, and I am surrounded by women of all different shapes and sizes. My Zumba class became a social experience, and it helped me stay in shape without even realising it.

The key is to find a type of exercise that you enjoy. You could try:

- Exercise classes, e.g. aerobics, Zumba, circuit
- The gym
- Team sports, e.g. netball, football, rugby, cricket, basketball
- Yoga or pilates
- Kick boxing
- Running/jogging
- Walking
- Hiking
- Swimming

These are just a few ideas, but there are countless more.

So, why is exercise so important?

- Helps to regulate your metabolism, so you maintain a healthy weight
- Helps to keep you mobile and free of aches and pains
- Regulates your mood and helps you feel more upbeat
- Helps with your sleep pattern
- Can lower blood pressure
- Improves your heart health and protects against serious issues occurring

- Can be a social activity, which boosts your mood even more
- Helps to prevent age-related issue, such a dementia
- Helps prevent against type II diabetes
- Helps you to focus

As you can see, there aren't a lot of downsides to making exercise a regular part of your routine!

The ironic thing is that exercising will boost your mood and make you feel lighter and more confident overall. This is a fantastic way to feel more body confident, and you will be toned and healthier as a result.

The bottom line to remember from this chapter, and actually from this book overall? Your health should come first.

Chapter 6: Different Body Shapes, and How to Dress For Yours

We have mentioned a few times throughout the book about dressing for your body shape, your style, and your appearance. We have said time and time again that you shouldn't compare yourself to anyone else, and you should dress for your style and body shape.

But, how do you identify what your body shape is?

Female Body Shapes

Hourglass – Curvy, small waist, you literally curve out at the breast area, in at the waist, and back out again at the hips. If your hips are around the same width as your shoulders, you have an hourglass body shape.

An hourglass body shape should not be hiding those killer curves! You need to emphasise them, not hide them, and you can do this with belts to perfection. Try a long belted jumper, or a pencil skirt, you don't want to cover your curves with too much bagginess, you need to show off what you have. Wrap dresses are also the hourglass girl's best friend, because it highlights what you want it to highlight and skims over what you might not be comfortable with. Wide legged trousers are also a great idea. Perfect!

Apple – Slim legs and bottom half, but carries weight around the middle. This means you are an apple body shape.

The best course of action to dress an apple body shape is to try and take the attention away from your middle portion and instead turn attention to your shoulders and your fantastic legs! To do that you could try a swing coat, which brings your body back into proportion, or a skater-type skirt, which doesn't cling, and instead gives the illusion of an hourglass type of shape. Shift dresses are another thing to try, which skim over the mid-section, or perhaps a pair of straight leg pants, which sit low on the hips, to avoid highlighting the mid-section.

Banana – In-keeping with the fruit theme, if you are not very curvy, and your hips are basically the same width as your waist, you are a banana body shape.

To dress this type of body shape you should be aiming to highlight your tiny waist (many people would love a tiny waist, so rock it!), and you should also be aiming to create the appearance of a larger chest area. To do this, ruffles are your friend! A ruffled top will give the illusion of curves. A jacket which is slightly loose but has a band around the bottom, clinging to your hips, will again help to create a more curvy look on your top half. A dress with the sides cut out was literally made for your body shape!

Pear – If you have wide hips, which are wider than any other part of your body, you are a pear shape. This is one of the most common body types.

The key with a pear shape is to create balance, so you need to give the illusion of a longer torso, and turn the attention to your top half, not the bottom half. This season's off the shoulder flare tops are ideal for this type of body shape, so think gypsy tops, giving you the perfect summer festival look. An A line skirt is a good choice, because this highlights your waist, and then flares out where your hips begin, rather than clinging. Remember I mentioned my sister rocking boot cut trousers? That is because she is a pear shape, and they look wonderful on this body shape.

Male Body Shapes

Rhomboid – If you have broad shoulders and narrow hips and waist, you are a rhomboid body type.

The good news? Most clothes fit this type of shape, so you're in luck! The key is to keep your entire body in proportion, so whilst they're not likely to make a huge fashion comeback, avoid flared trousers, and instead think tailored suits and trousers, slim fitting shirts and tops. You can also easily try patterns and checks, without worrying about creating a larger portion of your body. We're dealing with proportions here.

Inverted triangle – If you have broad shoulders, but your waist and hips are narrow, you are an inverted triangle shape (an upside down triangle).

This type of body shape needs to bear in mind that there is a difference in balance between the shoulders and hips. To pull it all back into shape, consider adding a belt to break up your outfit, go for V neck tops, and try double-breasted suit jackets, or general jackets, because it will give the illusion of a wider torso.

Rectangle – This type of body shape has shoulders and waist which are in proportion, but are narrow.

A good idea with this body shape is to try and widen the illusion of the shoulders and you can do that by going for jackets that are structured or shoulder padded, layering your clothes to create a wider chest, and opting for necklines which are circular, to keep the eye attention upwards.

Triangle – A little like the female pear shape, a male triangle has wider hips and waist than the shoulders.

To pull proportions back in, avoid anything too baggy, because it will just drown you out, and instead, stick to well-fitting, tailored clothes. Dark colours on the top half are also ultra-flattering, as well as single breasted, button down shirts. If you're going for stripes, stick to vertical or pinstripes.

Oval – An oval body type has narrow shoulders and slim legs, but a wider stomach area. This is hugely common.

To dress an oval body shape, try and wear vertical stripes or pinstripes, which will give the illusion of height, and also stick to well-tailored clothes which fit well, and don't go towards the side of being too baggy. Dark colours are a good idea also.

As you can see, there are many different body types, and you might find that you don't even fit into one with perfection. In that case, take advice from both types you are bordering on, to create the perfect balance for your shape.

Dressing for your body shape is basically key to looking fantastic with what you have, and being ultra-body confident as a result!

Conclusion

How are you feeling now you have read this book? Are you feeling lighter and more confident?

That is the aim!

The one thing I wanted to instil into anyone who reads this book is the importance of being happy in your own skin. This isn't about rocking the latest trends, it's not about being hugely fashionable, and it's not even about flaunting your body on the beach; it's about being healthy and content with whatever shape you have. Obviously, if you need to make changes, do them for you and for your health, but other than that, it's a mindset thing which needs to be changed in order for you to be happy and free of body confidence demons.

If that little devil on your shoulder rears its ugly head every now and then, be safe in the knowledge that this is normal, and it's doesn't mean that you're failing. Nobody can be 100% body confident, 100% of the time, but we can strive to be as confident as possible. If you have a wobble, that's fine; simply feel it, acknowledge it, turn it into a positive, bin it, and move on. You are a human being, and human beings are intrinsically flawed when it comes to being hugely positive all the time! The key is in how you deal with it.

The first step now lies with you. Identify what your particular trigger is, and then you can work to minimise it, and eventually kick it out of your life for good. This is going to take time, it's going to take effort, but it will be one of the most worthwhile things you will ever do in your life.

Body confidence, when it is at its lowest, can ruin your life. Do you think life is too short to be worrying about your love handles? I do!

I wish you the best of luck on your journey towards optimum body confidence; if I can do it, anyone can!

Thank you for reading my book.

I would love it if you could leave me an honest review on what you thought of this book.

If you like to know more about my books and the opportunity to be notified of free promotions please visit www.arylapublishing.com website

*Or follow **Aryla Publishing** on*

Facebook

Twitter

Instagram

Thank you

Please see other Titles from

ARYLA PUBLISHING Visit

www.arylapublishing.com

to sign up for new release books and free promotions

Children's Books

The Body Goo Series

The Billy Series

The Ruby Series

Emergency Services

Love Bugs and Animals

Adult Books

Self Help Books

Diet and Wellbeing

Comedy Books

Romance Books

Other Publications

How to be a World Leader – By Tyler Moses (Comedy)

The year is 2017 and while none of us know what the future will hold at present we are at the mercy of a world leader in the USA that did not seem possible. But it has happened some ask how? Some ask why? But there is support out there so I say if he can do it then so can I and so can you!

If you are not automatically born into it and lucky enough to be an heir to a kingdom (we will also cover how to bump yourself up the ranks) if you have the unfortunate sibling line to contend with that does not put you in prime position.

In the world, we live in today with technology at our fingertips we have more control and access to information so make use of it the world is your oyster if you have visions of being the most powerful person in the world and have an unstoppable ego then this could be the job for you.

Keeping Your Children Safe – By Fiona Welsh (Self Help – Business)

Without a doubt, the most important and treasured things we have in our lives are our children. We give birth to them, we raise them, we worry about them, and we love them to the end of the world and back again. It is no surprise that when we see worrying events on the news, it first makes us think of our children.

We can't protect our kids from everything in life, and we can't shield them from the things that are going on around the globe, but we can do our very best to keep them as safe as possible. As a parent you will no doubt be very familiar with the thought that you want to wrap your children up in cotton wool and avert their eyes from anything that isn't Disney magical. Things can and do happen, but part of the solution is to know how to teach your children about safety in general, in the right way. Learning to show them that it is fine to explore, fine to live, but that being on the lookout for danger is vital.

So, how do you do that? How do you tread that fine line between living life and avoiding dangerous situations?

<u>How to Make Money Online</u> –
By Fiona Welsh (Self Help – Business)

Unfortunately, the pot of gold at the end of the rainbow is yet to be found, there doesn't seem to be a Leprechaun smiling at whoever manages to stumble upon this long-famed prize, and as for the money tree, well, it's still as elusive as ever.

From time to time, we all find money hard to come by, and no matter how hard we work, or how much we save, it's likely that there are things we want and need that we can't afford at the present time. Obviously, that doesn't mean that your money situation is going to be difficult all the time, because cash flow ebbs and flows (pardon the pun) as much as anything in life, but finding ways to help it along a little is always a good thing.

The internet has changed so much about our modern-day lives, it is quite hard to think of anything that we don't use an online connection for in some way or another. From booking holidays, doing our grocery shopping, meeting the new Mr or Mrs Right in our lives, or finding a new job, the Internet connects it all. So, taking that thought a little further, can the Internet help us to earn a little extra cash when our flow isn't, well, flowing as fast as we would like?

Of course, it can!

The Internet is a fantastic place to start, and the beauty of all of it is that you can do it from the comfort of your armchair!

Julia's Dilemma – By Lyndsey Carter (Romantic Comedy)

Julia sighed as she stepped onto the escalator. As it moved and took her up, she sighed again. Another boring day and another crammed ride home on a smelly train with no seats. She longed for some excitement, something to shake things up. She was sick of the same old, same old.

Julie boarded the train, already knowing as she craned her neck to scan each corner that there would not be any seats open. Instead, she settled for a hand-hold on the pole near the back wall. But her surroundings ceased to bother her as she stared off into the distance and let her thoughts roam. She looked at the houses she passed and imagined what type of people lived there. The train line ran at the back of the houses giving Julie a view of the garden. Some gardens had washing hanging up; others had kids' toys. Some gardens were overgrown like a mini jungle. It was a little daydream game Julie liked to play when she didn't have a book or paper to read. Soon the passing gardens and motion of the train made her eyes heavy.

Julia fought to keep her eyes open, scared that she would miss her stop. Even after six years of riding the same train back and forth to work, she was still afraid that she would fall asleep and ride until the train reached the end of the line.

The mechanical voice announced the train's next stop, and that was enough to wake Julia. She elbowed her way to the front door and stood with the other people who always got off at this stop.

We also have a selection of Adult Coloring Books to help relax pass the time and de-stress.

Beautiful Illustrations and puzzles in the back for your entertainment.